To Inspire You!...

AN INSPIRING WORK OF POETRY
FILLED WITH SPIRITUAL MESSAGES OF HOPE.

BY
LINDA M. D. QUEEN

To Inspire You!...

Copyright 1998 L.M.D. Queen

Inquiries concerning speaking engagements or bulk orders of this book should be addressed to:
>Linda Queen
>5503 Wilvan Road
>Baltimore, Maryland 21207

ISBN 0-9636042-2-X
1. Poetry 2. Inspirational 3. Self Help I. Title
Published by: Clark Associated Businesses
P.O. Box 50178
Baltimore, Maryland 21211

All rights reserved. This publication cannot be reproduced, transmitted, photocopied or recorded without the written consent of the author.

Printed in the United States of America
Book Design By Keith Eric Costley

*THIS BOOK IS DEDICATED TO MY PRECIOUS
AND DEAR MOTHER, JOAN QUEEN. I LOVE YOU!*

TO INSPIRE YOU!...

ACKNOWLEDGEMENTS:

First, I give honor to my Lord and Saviour Jesus Christ, for without him, I could do and would be nothing; to my pastor, Bishop David W. Spann, Sr. who has stood by me and greatly encouraged me to live a Holy Life! Thank you Bishop Spann! I also thank you for not giving up on me; to Mother Spann and my entire Church Family of the Greater Remnant Church of God in Christ; to my dear mother, Ms. Joan Queen, who mean so much to me, I am here today because of her, thank you for being a "True" MOM and for loving me . . . "In-Spite-Of; you are the greatest! To my precious Grandmothers, Ms. Pauline Brown and Ms. Gladys Middleton; to my Dad, Mr. James Queen; to my sister and brothers Brenda Williams, Thomas Hill, Kenneth Hill, James Queen and Dewayne Queen; to all my family and dear friends that have made even the slightest difference in my life; I Love You All! To Michael Clark who encouraged me to write and made this book possible - I thank you. The truth is that there are so many people who have helped me along the way. I cannot name them all, but know that I thank you. May God Bless and Keep You All!

TO INSPIRE YOU!...

INTRODUCTION

*One day while I was in church,
I heard a poem being read,
then when I went home that day
I thought about what the poem said.
You can surely touch someone's heart I thought,
by reading a poem or two.
But be careful you must be led by God,
in whatever you do.
I asked the Lord to give me a title of a poem to write,
To my surprise, He touch my mind and
gave me these poems,
I pray that they will be an encouragement
to your life!*

TO INSPIRE YOU!...

HOLD ON YOUNG PEOPLE ... GOD LOVES YOU

Hold to God's unchanging hand , for there is temptation all around,
And young people please hold on even though peer pressure may sometimes abound,
God's way is the best way for you and for me, so on God let's get hooked,
Don't be fooled, there's only one way to make it, to obey God's word, so don't fail to "Do the Book",
Take a stand for what is right and know that God will surely stand with you,
And if you ever feel discouraged by troubles, look unto God, He will see you through,
Ask Him for guidance, direction, and at the crossroads, seek God for the way to take,
And God will bless you greatly, He knows what's best for you, remember you can trust God for His promises, He won't break.

TO INSPIRE YOU!...

PLEASE, TURN YOUR LIFE AROUND!
(Dedicated to my dear brother, "Buck")

I hurt, oh how I hurt, it's so hard for me to bear this pain,
Oh Lord, what can I now do, now that I realize the life I lived was all in vain,
What have I gained, what have I accomplished, but misery, suffering and depression,
If I could only turn back the clock, I'd do things different, for I've learned a hard lesson.
Oh drug addicts, put down the drugs while you can and have your strength,
'Cause it's not worth the outcome, no it's not worth dying for, so please stop while your life you can add length!
Oh, I can't begin to tell you how terrible this pain is for me,
So please don't go down that same road, let Christ set you free!

TO INSPIRE YOU!...

The high cost of low living is what it is in a nutshell,
For it cost to live this life also, but it's not worth it, believe me when I tell,
Here my cry O' God and deliver my soul from sin,
And I will be a witness unto you, and tell of your goodness unto men,
No, I don't have to die this way, you can bless me to live,
I must warn others to stop while they can and to you their lives to give,
Raise me from this pit, how great the wages of sin, oh, how great!
But God, I'm in your hands now, let your will be done, please don't let it be said ...It's Too Late!!!

TO INSPIRE YOU!...

BEAUTY IS . . .

*So, you don't think you're beautiful because
  of what you feel you're lacking,
And you feel as though you were cheated and
  in some physical way you're slacking,
Don't let this world fool you and have you
  thinking that beauty is in your figure,
Because if you do, you'll always wish you were
  smaller and in some cases . . . bigger!*

*True beauty is not in our outward appearances
  at all,
True beauty is not whether you're rich, poor,
  black, white, big, little, short or tall!
You see, we all can be beautiful if we really know
  what true beauty is at it's best,
True beauty is loving the Lord and living a life
  of holiness!!!*

TRUE BEAUTY IS BEING HOLY!!!

TO INSPIRE YOU!...

WAIT ON THE LORD

Wait on the Lord and be of good courage,
Whether it's for deliverance, a job situation or perhaps even marriage,
My God shall supply our every need while we wait,
Truly it's time to trust and live for the Lord before its everlasting too late!

What shall I render unto God for all of His benefits towards me,
My life, my hope, my trust, my all Lord, I surrender unto thee!!
You see, I found out that life is so much better when we serve our Lord,
So you see, it's well worth the wait . . . and it's for our good . . . so wait, I say, on the Lord!!!

TO INSPIRE YOU!...

A FRIEND IS . . .

Someone who really cares about everything you do,
They'll help you and support you and will always
see you through,
Someone who will come when called, anytime
of the day,
To try to meet your need and help in any way!

A friend not only comes if he or she is well,
But even when they're sick, they'll be there
just as well,
A friend is not only there just because you
have some money,
They'll even be there when you're broke, whether
it's rainy, snowy or sunny!

Someone who will stick with you until the
very end,
And share your joy, heartaches and pain . . .
now that's a friend!
Someone who'll still be around even when
you're sad,
But remember, you'll never lose a friend if
truly one you had!

TO INSPIRE YOU!...

*A friend will not run from your troubles, but will
   share them instead,
They will not try to keep you down, just so they
   can get ahead,
A friend will always be there to help you, no
   matter what condition you're in,
I'm so glad I know that JESUS is that kind of
   FRIEND!*

GOD IS IN CONTROL

*God is in control saints, no matter how far He
   seems to be away,
Don't let nothing separate you from His love,
   goodness and grace,
I'm so glad with every dark night there's a bright
   sunny day,
But what you have to always do is to READ, FAST
   and PRAY!!!*

TO INSPIRE YOU!...

O' GIVE THANKS

O' give thanks unto the Lord, call upon His name,

O' give thanks unto the Lord, for the sunshine as well as the rain,

O' give thanks unto the Lord, for His goodness and wonderful works towards men,

O' give thanks unto the Lord, for bringing us out of sin!

O' give thanks unto the Lord, for it is a good thing for us to do,

O' give thanks unto the Lord, for the many times he brought us through!

O' give thanks unto the Lord, each and every day,

Lord help us to always be grateful for everything O Lord we Pray!

TO INSPIRE YOU!...

FOR A FRIEND

As we travel down life's highway and meet nice friends along the way,
Friends who will encourage you and help you make it through each and every day!

We should stop and take the time, to show our appreciation and gratitude,
For all the gifts and blessings that come our way through friends like you!
If everyone were as thoughtful, kind and considerate as you are to me,
This world would be by far, a better place for us to be!

This small note of "Thank You" goes out to you from my heart,
To let you know how much I appreciate your friendship from the very start!

TO INSPIRE YOU!...

PRONE TO WANDER!

*Why are we so prone to wander far from
   God above,
When He has done so much for us, even sent His
   son to die . . . just to show His LOVE!
O' Lord, help us not to stray from your will
   or from your way,
Keep us everyday Lord, in your holy and perfect
   will, we pray!*

*Forgive us Lord for all our sins and help us
   to sin no more,
And Lord help us to keep our minds on thee,
   for only You can restore!
Dear Lord thank you for your grace and mercy,
   for granted we should not take it,
For we realize that living holy and according to
   your word is the only way we'll make it!*

TO INSPIRE YOU!...

DON'T GIVE UP!

*While in the storm of life, we walk going
 through troubles and fears,
Always remember not to give up for Jesus
 is ever so near!
Just hold on my friend and keep the faith
 for God will carry you through,
But we must not quit, we must not stop
 for God is watching you!!*

*"Good things come to those that wait"
 is something to think about,
And the Bible state to "wait on the Lord,"
 He'll be there without a doubt!
It's so important to hold on to God and
 his unchanging hand,
And also to remain faithful in everything
 we do, for it is God's Command!!!*

TO INSPIRE YOU!...

RETIRING?

When all the years of working seem to have quickly passed by,
And you come to the point in your life when it's time to say goodbye . . .
Do take good care of yourself as you start each new day,
And may the Lord bless and keep you in good health, I pray!
Just a few lines to say farewell and wish you all the best,
And in the coming years may the Lord grant you happiness!!!

TO INSPIRE YOU!...

*IT MAY BE HARD
. . . BUT YOU CAN MAKE IT*

*Yes, I know that it is hard sometimes when
 you really make your mind up to serve GOD,
But I also know that He's done so much for me,
 and I'm gonna serve Him, no matter how hard!
The good always outweighs the bad in my life,
 and for this Lord, I thank thee!
O' Lord, my God, please help me to be the person
 that you created me to be!*

*Sometimes the burdens get heavy, and it seems
 so hard to bear,
But Lord, I know that I can make it through,
 because you are always there!
I'm so glad my mind is made up to serve you
 until I die,
For I'm grateful for all the things you've done
 for me, and I know when no one else is there,
 on you I can rely!!!*

*Thank you Lord for being so good, so merciful,
 kind, loving and true,
You're right there whenever I need you, you
 are everything to me . . . Lord, I Love You!!!*

TO INSPIRE YOU!...

SUCCESS IS . . .

*Success comes from our God above,
So, we must try to abide in His Love,*

*Under His care only is found true success,
Unto thee O' Lord, will I render my best,*

*Carefully planning to reach my goals,
Can't underestimate the importance of reaching lost souls,*

*Casting all my cares upon the Lord,
'cause it's only in thee will I be successful;
therefore, I must obey your word!*

*Everyday I'll give thanks and ask you to guide me through the day,
Each step I take, please be with me and keep me in your will, I pray!*

*Steadfast, unmovable and faithful to you, I'll always be,
Standing on your word while I reach my full potential, Lord help me.*

*So to me to be successful, we must put God first in everything we do,
Surely, if we do this and stay faithful to God, He will see us through!!!*

TO INSPIRE YOU!...

I'M NOT THAT WAY

*Please try to get to know me, before you
 put me down or draw your own conclusion,
Because what you think may just be wrong,
 but I'm no illusion!
I'm just a child of God who's trying my best
 to do the right things in life,
Oh no I'm not perfect . . . made many mistakes,
 but dear Lord, please help me to do what's right!
So many people may judge me wrong, and say I
 am things that I'm not,
You should really get to know someone before you
 judge or criticize them . . . you may find you'll
 like them a lot!
Tis such a shame some may even dislike me before
 I've had anything to say,
Take some time and get to know me, you'll soon
 find that the way you first thought . . . no, I'm
 not that way!*

TO INSPIRE YOU!...

DON'T LET NO ONE STOP YOU!

Don't let no one stop you from reaching your goal,
Don't let no one interfere with the saving of
  your soul,
When your mind's made up to move ahead in life,
You will surely be faced with obstacles, but you
  must stand and fight!
Hold on to your dream, never ever give up or quit,
You can make it, you can make it, you can make
  it, You - Can - Make - It!
Although I've been hindered and I've been slack,
Now it's time for me to move ahead, I must
  fight back!
I'm not a quitter, I'm no fool, and I'm no door
  mat, no not me,
Satan, I command you in the name of the Lord,
  to drop your weapon and flee!
It's time I move up and ahead to fulfill my dreams
  and goals in this life,
And I won't let no one stop me anymore from
  doing what I know is right!

TO INSPIRE YOU!...

ALL IS VAIN, EXCEPT IT BE FOR GOD!

Vanity of Vanities, all is vain except it be done in the will of God,
Oh Lord, our Father, help us to always be on our guard,
Against Satan and all of his traps and his ways,
For you have already ordered our steps to take each and everyday,
Lord, help us to follow what has already been ordered by you,
And with your help Lord, come what may in life - we will surely make it through!

TO INSPIRE YOU!...

YOU CAN'T KEEP ME DOWN!

Go ahead, look me up and down with your frown, talk about me if you please, but that won't keep me down,

Go ahead, make fun of me for being lean, try to get me upset by being so mean, but that won't keep me down!

Go ahead, tell lies on me if you got the gall, laugh at me when I may fall and have my back against the wall, but that won't keep me down!

Go ahead, scandalize my name, try to put me to shame and stop me from reaching fame, but that won't keep me down!

Pick on me if you like, do things against me just for spite and for no reason hate me with all your might, but that won't keep down!

Smile at me to my face and then turn around and spread rumors about me all over the place, while all the time trying to make me feel that you're my ace, but that won't keep me down!

TO INSPIRE YOU!...

Try to stop me from moving ahead, even sometimes wishing that I was dead, oh quit acting like a kid, 'cause you can't keep me down!
Wanting me to get nowhere . . . to have nothing . . . to be nothing, just because you don't care, but that won't keep me down!

I'll just blossom as a rose, as God's blessing on my life unfolds - oh wait a minute, don't you know- you can't keep me down!
I'll learn to love you just the same, I'll pray real hard to reach that aim, you can't stop me, but only help me to gain . . . 'cause you can't keep me down!
Oh no, I'm far from perfection, got a very long way to go, but why don't you want me to grow, doing anything you can to keep me low, be a friend and not a foe, 'cause you can't keep me down!
Stop trying to stop me from being all that I can be, ask the Lord to set you free, don't be bound, don't you see . . . a child of God - you can't keep down!

TO INSPIRE YOU!...

LORD, I THANK YOU

Lord, I just want to thank you for all that you have done for me,
You have blessed me in so many ways and I just want to thank and praise thee!
Sometimes it's so easy not to thank the Lord as we should,
But it really should be hard not to, for He has been so good!!!
I realize if we take more time to thank Him, for the things He has done,
He'll certainly look on our needs, and He'll take care of them, each and every one!

TO INSPIRE YOU!...

FOR THE YOUTH

Young people yield yourself to God,
And remember that God is always near and
  ready to help even when the road gets hard,
You are never too young for God to bless and
  use you,
But you must be willing to be a vessel for God
  to work through you,
O' God we thank you for our parents who care
  and love us very much,
For your word says to honor our mother and
  father, and with long life you'll reward us!
Lord, help us to be obedient to your work, and
  to abide in your holy will,
So we may grow into what you have us to be,
  and when we are faced with temptations, give
  us the strength we need to "Be Still".

TO INSPIRE YOU!...

A MOTHER'S DAY POEM

Happy Mother's Day to all of you, and wishing you the best,
May all your days be filled with love, joy, peace and happiness!
You are very special people and no one could ever take your place,
So please take good care of yourselves and may God always give you grace,
To be strong, patient, and long suffering through each trail a child may bring,
For no one on earth deserves this day more; no, not even a king!

A Mother is there when all others fail to encourage you along the way,
A Mother will love until the end and more with each passing day!
A Mother will say "hold on" when all others will say "quit,"
A Mother will stick by your side, or be by your side with a stick!
A Mother's love is unconditional, she'll love you "anyway,"

TO INSPIRE YOU!...

*Tis such a shame it's only once a year, when it
should be everyday!!*
*A Mother's love is unconditional, she'll love you
in spite of,*
*The only greater love than a mother's is the love
from our God above!!*

DRAW ME NEARER . . .

*Draw me nearer, nearer Precious Lord to the
cross where thou has died,*
*And I'll be forever alright as long as I make
you my guide!*
*Oh, how I long to get to know you more and
more, day by day,*
*Oh, the comfort I have in knowing you are
with me, come what may!*
*Such love you have for me, none else could
ever compare,*
*Such grace and mercy you have bestowed, Oh,
how much you care!*

TO INSPIRE YOU!...

WHY SHOULD I SETTLE FOR LESS

Why should I settle for less when God has what's best for me,
Why should I fail every test, when God can and will strengthen me!
Why should I allow the troubles of this life get me down and depressed,
When God is able to supply all my needs and remove all strife, and all He requires from me is a "completely yes."
Why, Oh tell me why should I settle for less, when God is the best thing that ever happened to me,
He has so much more than this world could ever offer to me,

GOD HAS THE VERY BEST!

TO INSPIRE YOU!...

NO EXCUSE!

*No excuse, if I don't make it to Heaven,
no excuse at all,
No excuse I'll have for Jesus, If I don't
fulfill my call,
No excuse for me because God has made
the way,
No excuse I'll have to render; after all,
what could I say???*

*God saved me, sanctified me, and filled
me with His spirit,
God gave me many chances to get right,
many . . . I must admit it!
God gave me my right mind and snatched
me from the hands of death,
God gave me joy and peace, and when I
was sick . . . He restored my health!
God took away the drugs and alcohol, and
gave me peace within,
God gave me love and showed me He cared
for me when He freed me from sin!
God gave me new life and when I was bound,
God set me free,
What excuse could I have when He's done so
much - no, there will be no excuse for me!!!*

TO INSPIRE YOU!...

WAKE UP!

You think he loves you, you think he cares?
Then, why is it that every time you really need him,
　that so - called man of yours is never there?
Yeah, he says all kinds of nice things to you just
　to get his way,
And when you know things are not right,
　don't let him make you think everything's Okay.

Wake up and see that he means you no good
　at all,
Put that man out of your life, 'cause all he does
　is make you fall!
Get right with God and let Him bless you, 'cause
　God will supply your every need,
You don't need anyone that tries to uproot you
　from God's seed!

Look in the mirror and know that you are
　wondrously made by God,
And tell that man you don't need him "messing
　up" your life anymore because you're a child of
　the King ". . . even if it's hard,"
God will richly bless you and show you Love, Joy
　and Peace in which none can compare,
And if you put God first, He'll add unto you, just
　wait and see . . . come on now because
　God REALLY cares!!!

TO INSPIRE YOU!...

DO THE RIGHT THING!

Lord, help me to do that which is pleasing in your sight,
And I'll promise to do my best to love and serve you with all my might!
Temptations sometimes come and try to turn me from your will,
But Lord, give me the strength to stand and in your will help me to be still!

Thank you for forgiving me for all the wrong that I have done,
But now it's time for me to do the right things and your race I'll run!
There is none like you Lord, the love you give like no other,
Help me to have that love for all of my sisters and my brothers!

We must do the right things while daylight is still here,
And if you ever have a doubt or a problem, call on God He's always near!
It'll be worth it all when we see Jesus, Our Saviour, Lord and King,
Lord, hear our cry, for we want to live for you, please help us to "Do The Right Thing!!"

TO INSPIRE YOU!...

TRUST GOD

*When things go wrong as they sometimes will
 . . . trust God,
Know that everything will be alright if we only
 keep still . . . trust God,
The Bible tells us to "Be still and know that I
 am God" . . . trust God,
For we know that for God, there is nothing too
 hard . . . trust God,*

*Even when we don't see our way, Lord we know
 that you are there . . . trust God,
Our burdens, heartaches, trials and disappoint-
 ments, you will help us to bear . . . trust God,
When the way is not clear . . . trust God,
When we know that we know, when we truly put
 our trust in you, we have nothing to fear . . .
 TRUST GOD!*

TO INSPIRE YOU!...

DON'T BE FOOLED!

*Don't be fooled by thinking the grass is greener
on the other side,
Don't let the foolish ways of this ole world be
your guide,
How can you think that it can be better without
Christ in your life,
When all you'll end up with while you're alive
is pain, misery and strife!*

*Don't be fooled by thinking "you are missing
out on something good,"
When all the best things come from Christ, if
you serve Him as you should!
And no, please don't forget the many many
blessings that Christ has bestowed on you,
For if you do, you'll live beneath your privilege
and miss out on Heaven's rewards too!*

TO INSPIRE YOU!...

FOR MY MOM . . .
YOU WERE THERE . . .

*When I had no one else to talk to,
 you were there for me,
When I needed support and comfort,
 you were there with me,
When I needed a shoulder to lean on,
 you were there by me,
When I felt so all alone, disappointed or
 disheartened, you were there near me,*

*Mother, thank you for your love that you
 have not failed to show,
Thank you for your compassion for it has
 helped me to grow,
Thank you for all the times that you gave
 me your hearing ear,
Thank you for all the wonderful things you
 have done for me year after year,*

TO INSPIRE YOU!...

*Even though at one time in our lives, we
    were very far apart,
But now God has brought us together by giving
    us more love for each other in our hearts!
I know you always wish you could do so much
    more for me,
But mom, don't you worry . . . God will provide
    . . . just you wait and see!*

*You are the greatest mom that ever lived in the
    whole wide world,
You're more precious than silver or gold,
    diamonds, rubies and pearls!
I love you so very much mom, this I want you
    to know,
And I'm so grateful for all you've done and
    desire to do mom, no one could ever take your
    place down here below!!!*

YOU ARE THE GREATEST!!!

TO INSPIRE YOU!...

THE UNFOLDING ROSE

*Just as a rose begins to unfold and show the
 beauty that's inside,
We live and grow and in time we're like that rose,
 for what's inside we no longer hide,*

*Each petal, so delicate to the touch, so fragile . . .
 it must be handled with care,
The rich qualities of living we once disregarded
 are now and forever there,*

*But beyond the rose there is a stem, with thorns
 which hurt to the touch,
You see, before beauty can fully bloom,
 we sometimes must go through so much!*

*But, it was there all the time, once so unnoticed,
 unseen, yet blooming away so beautifully,
Until one day my eyes came open, and I realized
 that all the time the beauty I've always longed
 for was right there surrounding me!*

TO INSPIRE YOU!...

LIVE FOR CHRIST

*It may not always be easy to travel down life's
   highway,*
*For the road sometimes gets rough, no matter
   what you do or say,*
*But as we continue this journey to live our lives
   as we may,*
*We must keep one thing in mind, we are certainly
   not here to stay!*
*One day it will all be over, no more disappointments,
   heartaches, or pain,*
*But, unless you live for Christ, you are living your
   life in vain!*
*For Christ is the solution to every problem big or
   small,*
*There is nothing too hard for God, He can surely
   handle them all!*
*Give all your worries to Jesus and He will work
   them out,*
*Just have faith and really believe without a
   shadow of a doubt,*
*You see, God really loves us and he wants us to
   love Him in return,*
*For if we do, we'll live forever, but if we don't
   we'll burn!!*

TO INSPIRE YOU!...

THIS OLE ARMY

*I'm proud to serve in this ole Army, just as proud
   as I can be,
I'll cherish this uniform as long as I live and wear
   it with dignity,
Although at times I'm faced with tough challenges
   and there are struggles along the way,
I'll always remember what I stand for, my God
   and my country, the good ole USA!*

*This ole Army may have its downs, but as for me,
   I'll do what's right,
I'll stand up for the rights and freedom for all, and
   I'll stand with all my might!
So, no matter what happens in this ole Army, no
   matter what one may do,
Just hold on to what is right, be a good example,
   for some young soul is watching you!*

*Many young soldiers tend to follow examples of
   others, so it behooves us to do the right things
   at all times,
And remember that no man is an island, we all
   need each other, so lets treat all men equal, for
   to win the war, it takes all kinds!
United we stand, divided we fall, so lets help
   (and not hinder) one to "be all they can be,"
For its only when you have accomplished these
   things that you can truly be proud to have
   served in "this Ole Army."*

TO INSPIRE YOU!...

DON'T CRY FOR ME

Don't cry for me; for you don't know,
I gave my life to Christ awhile ago!
I know you are hurting deep inside,
But, know that it's with Christ that I now abide!
I thank you for the love that you showed to me,
But, remember it was Christ that set me free.
I'm free from this world's grief, misery and pain,
I'm free from the sorrow this ole life can bring
I'm free from the temptations that try to bring
  me down,
I'm free from the trials of this life that can some-
  times have you bound.
I'm free to praise the lord forever more,
I'm free to continually thank Him for opening so
  many doors.
So, don't cry for me, Heaven is in my view,
Just give your life to Christ and you will
  get there too.
Don't cry for me, no don't you even weep,
You see, I'm not dead, no, I am just asleep.

TO INSPIRE YOU!...

DON'T YOU DARE

Don't you dare treat me like I'm a disease,
Just because its God, and not you that I aim to please,
Don't you dare look at me and turn the other way,
Just so you don't have to speak or even ask if I'm okay,
Don't you dare hold a grudge against me just because for right I stand,
And nothing less than right is what I demand!

How can you sleep at night knowing that you're so wrong?
For misjudging me for being so weak, and having me to prove I'm strong,
How can you walk around holding your head up high?
When all you really care about is how "you look, no matter what happens to the next girl or guy!
How can you consider yourself such a success?
What are you basing it on, how many you knocked down or how many you helped to progress?

TO INSPIRE YOU!...

*You expect one to follow the motto, "Be All You
    Can Be,"*
But how can we, when bad examples is all we see?
*You should be proud of the ones who are doing
    what is right,*
*Not just proud of the ones that hang out with you
    all night!*
You need to reconsider what you think is fair,
*But to treat me so bad because I stand for what is
    right . . . Don't You Dare!!!*

TO INSPIRE YOU!...

CHRISTMAS POEM I

*As we celebrate this Christmas Season,
    let's remember why this special holiday,
For Christ came to save us from our sins and to
    show us that we can live saved . . .
    come what may!
In times like these, we need a loving Saviour, to
    bring hope, joy, peace and love,
For no one can ever give a better gift than the
    gift that was sent from God above!
Merry Christmas everyone, and may all your days
    be bright,
Thank God for Jesus, for in the dark days, Jesus
    came to bring us light!!!*

TO INSPIRE YOU!...

CHRISTMAS POEM II

Joy to the world, the Lord has come,
Lord, please help me to fully receive you, for we
  don't want to be caught with our work undone!
Thank you for loving us so much that you came
  here just to die,
Oh God, no matter what this life may bring,
  on you we can always rely,
You came in such a way, so lowly and meek,
  yet a Great King,
You proved to us your power and through you we
  can do all things,
Merry Christmas Jesus,
  thank you for the love you show,
Merry Christmas everyone, and remember to take
  the Lord along with you everywhere you go!!!

TO INSPIRE YOU!...

AGAINST ALL ODDS

Who would have thought I'd come this far with so many obstacles in my way,
Who would have thought I'd be what I am today instead of living a life of decay,
God brought me this far, and without him, there is nothing I would be able to do,
But don't you know that God love us all, and what he's done for me,
he'll do the same for you!

I lived the "Street Life," doing anything and everything that was oh so wrong,
But God, I thank you for turning my life around, and in my heart you put a new song!
This message is to let you know that no matter what the situation, God can bless you to greatly succeed,
Yes, I am a witness that — Against All Odds — GOD can raise you up indeed!

TO INSPIRE YOU!...

*Just trust in Him and don't ever give up, for He
    will bring you out,
Against All Odds — He'll make a way for you —
    He'll do it without a doubt!
God's been so good and I love Him because inspite
    of myself, He continues to show He cares,
So even when it seems the odds are against you,
    God can and will bless you, so when you think
    of giving up —— DON'T YOU DARE!!!*

Q TO INSPIRE YOU!...

YOU CAN

You can succeed and reach your goal if only you never give up,
You can make it through the hard times even when you feel you're drinking from a bitter cup,
You can accomplish so many things if only the trials you bear,
You can rest assure that everything in your life will be alright, if only you give God your care!

You can look beyond the storm, and know that a brighter day is ahead,
You can turn your sorrows into joy, if you stop trying and let God fix it instead!
You can always look up and you'll never have to worry, if only you put your trust in God,
You can dry your weeping eyes, you don't have to cry now, for with God nothing is too hard!

TO INSPIRE YOU!...

HELP ME LORD!

*Help me Lord to do what's right that I may live
for thee,*
*Help me Lord, please help me Lord to be what
you have me to be!*
*Sometimes I'm hindered and get so weak until I
don't stand as I should,*
*But Lord, I know you can do all things,
please help me, if you would,*
*I want to be used by you,
I want your will done completely in my life,*
*But, I know that it's impossible to do your will if
I'm filled with envy and strife!*
*Deliver me from all the things that's not like you
in my mind and in my heart,*
*And I will freely do your will and from your way,
I'll never part!*

TO INSPIRE YOU!...

DON'T JUST STARE – HELP ME

I know you see me, you think I'm really bad,
You walk right by me like you don't care,
  and that makes me very sad,
I realize I'm involved in a lot of very bad habits,
But, if you don't stop to help me — who will —
you have the Lord, I don't I must admit,
Does He tell you to walk by those who don't live
  the way you think they should,
But, if only you took some time and cared for those
  that are not living so right —- it will surely do us
  some good!
If you continue to walk on by and not show us the
  love of God,
Then what example do we have? With no good
  example; for us to change will be really hard!
Just stop and think a minute about where He's
  brought you from,
You would be nothing without Him, so please
  don't look down on me, I just need to be
  introduced to God's Son!

TO INSPIRE YOU!...

I can change too with the help of people like you,
But how can you say you're saved and live for
  Jesus, if for people like me,
  there's nothing you would do!
Watch out now, God may raise me to be a witness
  unto you, and you just may need me one day,
So don't turn your nose up to me because I smell
  from having too much to drink last night;
  can't you see, I need to hear a word from
  the Lord,
  and if you help me —— I just may change my
  way!!!

TO INSPIRE YOU!...

COLORS . . .

Red, blue, green, purple and pink, these colors don't seem to matter too much,
And gray, peach, fuchsia, and orange are colors that don't make too much of a fuss,
But, when it come down to the skin that covers our blood, bones and internal parts,
It seems to make a world of difference, even though what really should matter is what's in our hearts.
God made and loves all of us no matter what color or race,
And what we should really be concerned about is what He will say when we behold His face!
Have we fed some hungry soul or gave some encouragement along the way,
Or do we just live to hurt others unlike our skin color, and do not care what we say,
Have we comforted some poor widow who lost everything she had,
Or have we tried everything we could to make others who are of "a different color" sad,
Have we witness to someone who in sin was dead,
Or are we knocking others out the way - who are of "a different color" just so we can get ahead!

TO INSPIRE YOU!...

I think everyone of us should all go back to the
Bible and read,
Because God does not judge us by our colors,
but by our every deed,
He will not say "Well Done" they White, Black,
Red, or Yellow one,"
He will not say "come on up my child, you are the
right color, my mansion for you is done",
He will say "Come, ye blessed of my Father,
inherit the kingdom prepared for you from the
foundation of the world,"
You see, it's not in the color,
but the work that will make you gain this pearl,
For He'll say I was an hungered and you gave me
meat,
I was thirsty and knew you not, and you gave me
drink and a place to rest my feet,
I was naked, and my body you did clothe,
When I was sick and in prison,
you visited and it was Me you consoled,
No matter what color you are, it's Jesus that
makes the difference,
So please let's all come together as one and love
one another as we should,
and our reward Jesus will recompense!

TO INSPIRE YOU!...

LEAVE ME ALONE
(For those who try to turn you from God)

Leave me alone man, can't you see I'm saved and sanctified,
So why are you trying to turn me around from the one who, for me and for you, He was crucified!

Leave me alone man, can't you see my way of life is a life of holiness,
So why are you trying to make me backslide, and replace my joy with a lot of stress!

Leave me alone woman, can't you see I don't want to gossip and backbite,
So please carry your talk somewhere else, 'cause I'm trying my best to live right,

Leave me alone woman, can't you see I'm happy with Jesus alone,
So why do you always try to match me up with someone in whom I don't condone!

Leave me alone my brother and sister, I know we are kin,
But, can't you see I've changed my life and don't want to go back to sin,

TO INSPIRE YOU!...

Leave me alone my brother and sister,
*   you know I love you, yes I do,*
But I must serve my God for He knows and loves
*   me best and what's wonderful is that He loves*
*   you too!*

Leave me alone pew pastor and please let the
*   preacher do his duty,*
If you don't want to listen, okay,
*   but don't try to hinder me!*

Leave me alone my suppose - to - be sister in the
*   Lord,*
Why is it that instead of encouraging me,
*   you bring me down,*
*   yet, we're suppose to be on one accord!*

Leave me alone each and everyone that try to stop
*   or discourage me from reaching my spiritual*
*   goal,*
If you don't want to serve God as you should,
*   that's on you —- God allowed us to choose,*
*   but as for me, there is nothing on earth worth*
*   me losing my soul!*

Q TO INSPIRE YOU!...

UNDERNEATH IT ALL

Oh, so you think the outside is important,
  and you don't even look within,
Would you rather have something that looks good
  to you from the outside,
  but on the inside is full of sin!?!
Stop putting all your cares and concerns in all the
  wrong places,
Are you really looking deep within or just
  concerned about the faces,
I'm so glad that God looks at the heart,
  and not on the outward appearance,
But don't worry if you're like this,
  just pray to God and He will give deliverance
You see, the best qualities are the ones that you
  can not see with your eyes,
For it may not be what you think anyway,
  for people can wear a disguise,
Lord, fix my heart that I may love right,
  and fix my mind to think right I pray,
And please help us not to be so judgmental on
  what we see, for we may just get in your way!

TO INSPIRE YOU!...

STAND

*Steadfast, unmoveable and always abounding in
   the work of the Lord is how we should always be,
So that we can be stable, faithful and a living
   witness unto the world for thee,*

*Tell of His goodness, tell of His mercy, tell of
   His kindness and His Love,
Tell of His Son who died for us after he came
   down from His throne above,*

*Always remember what God has done and
   where He has brought you from,
Always pray and remain in His will until His
   kingdom come,*

*Never ever allow no one or nothing to make you
   fall from His saving grace,
Nothing is more precious than pleasing God,
   nothing is worth losing this race,*

*Delight in the Lord and He will help us if we
   hold on to His unchanging hand,
Doing all the good we can and having done all
   . . . Let Us Stand!!!*

TO INSPIRE YOU!...

IS THE LORD IN?
I Kings 19:11-12

When trials and tribulation come into your life . . .
  Is the Lord in?
When the storms of life are raging over . . .
  Is the Lord in?
The wind, earthquake and the fire were not
  caused by the Lord,
But deliverance come in a still small voice which
  was His word,
Many things come to destroy and hinder us from
  running this race,
But don't let nothing stop you from seeing the
  master face!
Let the Lord in and give Him your all and all,
For He alone is the one who can pick us up when
  we fall!
So just because the wind, earthquake, and fire
  may come,
Does not necessarily mean that its something the
  Lord has done,
But there is one thing for sure and this is
  guaranteed,
If you let the Lord in, He will set you free!

TO INSPIRE YOU!...

ONE WAY

*Lord, help me to be one way at all times,
    instead of being up and down,
Help me not to be sometimes with a smile and
    sometimes with a frown,
Even though I may have good days and I may
    have bad days,
I realize that this is no excuse for a Christian to
    have such funny ways,
Help me to let nothing cause me to hurt anyone
    for acting "funny,"
And let my ways be the same when in my life its
    raining as well as when its sunny,
It's so important for us as Christians to let our
    light so shine at all times before men,
Because we never know when we can make a
    difference in someone else's life and bring them
    to Christ that they may be delivered from sin!*

TO INSPIRE YOU!...

IF YOU WANT ME, COME AND GET ME

You say you want me, you say you love me,
   but yet we're living different ways,
You tell me all the things you want from me,
   yet they're causing me to go astray,
You see God saved me a few years ago,
   and made my life anew,
And if you are serious enough about me,
   you'll let Him do the same for you,
I must confess, I have not been perfect or made a
   hundred on every test,
But one thing for sure,
   I realize I have been truly blessed!
Although I've fell and God forgave me,
   time and time again,
He does not keep giving me mercy just for me to
   sin,
At some point in our lives,
   we ought to be able to take a stand,
And go through our test without giving in or up,
   obeying Gods' command,
I've found God to be my everything,
   my need He does supply,

TO INSPIRE YOU!...

And on Him and Him only can we always rely,
So if you want me, come and get me,
   I'll be walking with the Lord,
For He has done too much for me,
   for me to turn against His word,
It's your choice, your own free will to do as you
   choose,
But as for me, as for my life,
   the Lord I cannot afford to lose!!!

TO INSPIRE YOU!...

WHEN YOU THINK EVERYTHING IS GOING WRONG . . .

*You're tired from working hard all day and
   church is about to begin,
You feel like pressing on but . . . your body tells
   you you're already at the end,
Your child is sick with the mumps and keeps
   crying for your attention,
You're all dressed and ready for church and can't
   wait to release some tension,
I wonder where could the ride be,
   he's suppose to be here by now,
Only God knows your every need,
   what you need, when, where and how,
So, your ride finally shows up and wondering
   why you're not gone,
Oops, your stockings just ripped and you're
   wondering what else could go wrong,
This poem is to let you know,
   that God is always near,
Through rain and shine, sun and storm,
   there's no need to fear,
Although at times nothing seems to be right,
   everything seems to go wrong,
But, always remember God has ALL power and
   read the 23rd Psalms!*

TO INSPIRE YOU!...

GOD'S WAY IS THE BEST WAY

*Though things of this world may look alright,
Though things that are wrong may sometimes
 seem right,
There's only one way in which to live,
And that's by God's word, our lives to give,*

*No matter how tempting the things of the world
 may seem,
Know that there's nothing greater than being
 redeemed,
Jesus is the light that shines in His children for
 all the world to see,
God's way is the best and only way for you and
 for me!!!*

TO INSPIRE YOU!...

COME TO JESUS

*Almost two thousands years ago on a hill called
   Mount Calvary,
Jesus died for us and in Him are we set free,
He did not die for His own personal gain,
But, He died so our living would not be in vain,
Just think of just how much God really loves us,
Truly He deserves in return our love and trust,
If today your blood is still running warm in your vein,
You ought to come to Jesus and in Him you'll reign,
Come to Jesus now while He can be found,
And if you're a backslider, it's time to turn back
   around,
Not matter what condition you may be in right now,
I'll guarantee He'll pick you up no matter how
   far you're down,
If you feel like you're sick and just can't get well,
God will heal your body, and you'll have a
   testimony to tell,
God can turn you around from any sinful habit,
Whether you're an alcoholic, thief, or drug addict,
God loves you even when you're living in sin,
But, it's time for you to love and live for Him,
   before your time comes to an end,
Not only be word of mouth, but by every deed,
In order to serve the Lord fully, you need to plant
   His seed!
It's time to give praise to whom praise is due,*

TO INSPIRE YOU!...

*To the Almighty Father in Heaven, and His son,
    Jesus too!*
*Call on Jesus for any Pneed you may have at this
    time,*
If you trust and believe,
    He'll help you and it won't cost a dime,
For we could have been dead and gone,
    but He still allow us to live,
He has shown us mercy, love and kindness,
    and has so much more to give,
But, the most important gift is the gift of salvation,
For without it, we would have eternal damnation,
Jesus can save you right now and set your soul free,
And in Him and Him only do we have the victory,
You might have problems on your present job,
You may have experienced some loss by being robbed,
*You may be going through some difficult times in
    your home,*
*Just always keep in your mind that God is still on
    the throne,*
Although it may seem sometimes that Jesus is far away,
Don't be blinded by persecutions,
    and please don't forget to pray,
God sees and He knows everything we go through,
*Just hold on and never doubt for God will surely
    bring you through!*

Q TO INSPIRE YOU!...

REMEMBER THE ROSE

There are times people may do you wrong and hurt you in more ways than one,

There are times you may want to give up on a "friendship" because all you can do to save it, you've done,

There was one time while I was overseas for my birthday, and surprisingly I received a bundle of roses and flowers from a friend,

I really appreciated them because I was really missing being home, missing my church, missing my kin,

When I began to think about how her words and actions sometimes did not make me feel as I thought they should,

I thought about the roses and flowers she had given me, then I realized it feels so much better to "think on the good",

We all say and do things sometimes that hurt others without really intending to,

But, when negative thoughts come to your mind about someone, this is what you should do,

Think about the good and don't let negative thoughts rule your mind,

TO INSPIRE YOU!...

Remember that God sees and hears everything...
   all of the time,
Positive thoughts are better for you and don't
   worry because everything that happens,
   God knows,
So when negative thoughts come to your mind . . .
   just remember the rose!

IN SEARCH OF

Sometimes we search until we find for a love
   that's true, whole and divine,
We ask ourselves, why so long is this love I'm
   searching for being prolonged?
But, it just might be that you need not to
   look anymore,
For true love comes from within, to love is to know
   God for He's knocking on your door,
And once you let Him in and allow Him to abide,
A love that's right for you, God will provide!
Let go and let God, for He knows what's best for you,
He knows just what you need, He loves you best
   and He's able to make a dream come true!

TO INSPIRE YOU!...

GIVE YOUR PROBLEMS TO GOD

*Oh what peace we often forfeit,
Oh what needless pain we bear,
All because we do not carry,
Everything to God in prayer!*

*God, how often do we suffer things that we really do not have to,
If we only let you work things out, for there is nothing that you can't do!
Please fix our hearts and fix our minds to always do that which is right,
And help us to turn all our problems over to you, for your yoke is easy and your burden is light!*

TO INSPIRE YOU!...

FROM MY HEART TO YOURS . . .

As we travel down life's highway and grow older each year,
We tend to realize more and more how much our loved ones are so dear,
So, I like to take this time right now to wish you all the best,
And may life have in store for you love, peace, joy and happiness!

HE WILL BRING YOU OUT!

Although the road right now may seem hard,
Hold on to your faith and trust in God!
Have no fear, don't despair and please don't you doubt,
For in God's own time, rest assure, He will surely bring you out!!!

Q TO INSPIRE YOU!...

DON'T BE DOWN — LOOK UP!

*Just a few lines to let you know whatever the
   problem may be,
Just turn it over to Jesus right now and He
   will set you free,
I don't like to see anyone sad, down, depressed
   or mad,
Especially when there is a God,
   who can make you glad!
God really loves you very much,
   and He's cares for you too,
For if He didn't, He would not have me write this
   poem to you!*

TO INSPIRE YOU!...

GETTING OLD

*God has blessed you with another year to grow
   a number older,
Now that you're the age you are, you should no
   longer need to cry on my shoulder!
This short message comes to tell you,
   you're not a baby anymore,
But, please don't get mad with me,
   and come knocking down my door!*

*Just be thankful and very grateful,
   you've reached the age that you are,
For at one time you were considered very young,
   but now you're passed that by far!
So, welcome to this brand new life of arthritis,
   aches and pains,
But, look on the bright side of things,
   at least you still remember your name!!!*

ABOUT THE AUTHOR

Linda Maureen Denise Queen was born in Baltimore, Maryland to James and Joan Queen. She attended Baltimore city public schools and the Community College of Baltimore. After a short time at the Community College of Baltimore, she enlisted in the Army Reserves. Two years after her enlistment she decided to move from the Reserves to "Active Duty." After several years in active duty, she returned to the Army Reserves where she is still enrolled today. She has recently completed an assignment overseas in support of "Operation Joint Guard." Her total experience exceeds sixteen years within the United States Armed Forces.

Linda Queen has traveled throughout the United States of America. She has also traveled overseas several times. As a result of her overseas tours, in the military, she has been able to visit numerous foreign countries and learn about various societies.

Ms. Queen states that the most important event that has ever happened in her life is when she gave her life to the Lord. She is very grateful to the Lord for allowing her to live long enough to make a change in her life. She indicates that she, loves the Lord with all of her heart, soul and mind. Currently, Ms. Queen is employed at Aberdeen Proving Grounds in Maryland, still serving in the army reserves. She has received numerous awards and recognitions throughout her military and civilian career for her professional and personal accomplishments.

She has a great concern for people. She especially loves children and always aspires to set a good example for them. One of her goals is to work more within the crime ridden and drug infested communities to help bring about a change. She desires to bring about a difference in the lives of those which whom she comes in contact, "just the same way God made it possible for her life to change." Ms. Queen's response to the question, "What can you do to make a difference?" was; "I'm not a professional psychologist, doctor, lawyer or teacher. I don't have a degree from any college or university. I was not born to a wealthy family. But, what I do have can make a big difference in the lives of those whom will receive it. I have the knowledge and experience of what God can do. God can take nothing and make something great. Don't ever feel that you are too bad, or too low to change. There is nothing too hard for God...and I'm a living witness to that!!!"

Ms. Queen currently resides in Baltimore, Maryland. She is single and does not have children. Her hobbies include: reading, writing, performing sign language and attending church services.